KEYS TO KINGDOMS: A GUIDE TO PROSPEROUS RENTAL PROPERTY INVESTING

KEYS TO KINGDOMS

A GUIDE TO PROSPEROUS RENTAL PROPERTY INVESTING

2

Contents

3

4

Presentation

Welcome to "Investment property Contributing: The most effective method to Make Riches and Recurring, automated revenue Through Shrewd Purchase and Hold Land Financial planning." Whether you're a carefully prepared financial backer hoping to grow your portfolio or a newbie anxious to set out on the excursion of abundance creation through land, this guide is intended to furnish you with the fundamental information and systems to prevail in the powerful universe of investment property contributing.

Motivation behind the Aide

Putting resources into investment properties can be a groundbreaking way to independence from the rat race, yet it requires cautious preparation, informed navigation, and a promise to long haul achievement. The goal of this guide is to give you the knowledge, tools, and step-by-step instructions you need to understand buy-and-hold real estate investing.

The Advantages of Investment property Contributing

Why pick investment properties? Past the potential for significant monetary profits, investment property contributing offers the chance to construct recurring sources of income, accomplish long haul appreciation, and lay out a powerful starting point for generational riches. As we dive into the different parts of this speculation procedure, you'll find how to outfit these advantages and relieve likely difficulties.

Setting Practical Assumptions

Prior to jumping into the particulars of market examination, property choice, and monetary methodologies, setting sensible expectations is critical. Land effective financial planning isn't an easy money scam, and achievement frequently requires persistence, steadiness, and a pledge to consistent learning. All through this aide, we'll stress the significance of figuring out your objectives, leading exhaustive examination, and settling on informed choices that line up with your one of a kind speculation targets.

As you leave on this excursion, recall that every property addresses a monetary resource as well as a potential chance to shape your monetary future. We should investigate the thrilling and compensating universe of investment property contributing together. Could it be said that you are prepared to transform properties into benefits? We should get everything rolling!

Section 1: Getting Started Real estate investing

Entails the strategic acquisition and management of properties in order to generate income and accumulate wealth. In this part, we'll cover the essential standards of land money management, including the sorts of properties, key wording, and the fundamental mechanics of how land can be a strong vehicle for monetary development.

Surveying Your Monetary Status

Before you set out on your land speculation venture, assessing your monetary situation is critical. You will be taken through a self-evaluation in this chapter to see if you are ready to invest in real estate. We'll investigate themes like credit wellbeing, reserve funds, and obligation the executives, helping you lay a strong monetary starting point for your venture tries.

Characterizing Your Speculation Objectives

Explaining your speculation objectives is a basic move toward building an effective land portfolio. In this part, we'll assist you with articulating your present moment and long haul targets. Whether you're looking for recurring, automated revenue, capital appreciation, or a mix of both, understanding your objectives will shape your speculation technique and impact property choice, funding choices, and by and large portfolio the board.

Keep in mind that there is no one-size-fits-all approach to real estate investing as we begin this journey. Your extraordinary monetary circumstance and goals will direct the choices you make en route. We should plunge into the basics of getting everything rolling on your way to turning into a sagacious and fruitful land financial backer.

Part 2: Statistical surveying and research

Identifying profitable business sectors the selection of the appropriate market is an essential component of successful land money management. In this part, we'll research the principles for recognizing markets significant solid areas for with for benefit. We'll dive into factors, for instance, people improvement, work markets, and money related pointers, helping you with pinpointing spots where land theories line up with your financial goals.

Dissecting Neighborhood Land Patterns

It is fundamental to have a comprehension of the elements of the nearby housing markets to make all around informed ventures. You will figure out how to examine patterns like market interest, rental rates, and property estimations in this part. By staying delicate to shifts in the local land scene, you'll be more ready to perceive important entryways and investigate potential hardships.

Directing a Near Market Examination (CMA)

A critical tool for determining a property's value in relation to its surrounding environment is the Near Market Examination (CMA). We'll walk you through the method for coordinating a CMA, covering key parts like comparative property decision, assessing strategies, and unraveling market data. This assessment will draw in you to make a lot of taught decisions while choosing the normal efficiency of a specific hypothesis property.

As we jump into measurable studying and assessment, recall that the ability to perceive promising business areas and grasp area designs is a skill that isolates viable land monetary sponsor. Could we outfit you with the data and gadgets to investigate the intricacies of market assessment and position yourself for progress in the domain of venture property contributing?

Section 3: Supporting Your Speculation

Investigating Home loan Choices

Getting the right supporting is essential in land effective money management. You will learn about the various mortgage options for financing your investment property in this chapter. We will investigate alternative financing options, government-backed loans, and conventional mortgages. Understanding the upsides and downsides of every choice will engage you to pick the funding structure those lines up with your speculation objectives.

Understanding Loan costs

Loan fees assume a critical part in the general expense of supporting and the benefit of your speculation. In this part, we'll demystify loan costs, talking about how still up in the air, factors that impact them, and methodologies for getting positive rates. A reasonable comprehension of financing costs will empower you to settle on informed choices while choosing a credit and dealing with your speculation's monetary elements.

Credit Endorsement Interaction

Exploring the credit endorsement interaction can be complicated, yet understanding the means included is pivotal for an effective land venture. We'll separate the advance application process, from social event fundamental documentation to working with loan specialists and going through the guaranteeing system. Toward the finish of this section, you'll have a complete comprehension of the stuff to get supporting for your speculation property.

As we dig into the domain of funding, remember that the right monetary construction can essentially influence your profit from venture. Whether you're a first-time financial backer or hoping to grow your portfolio, dominating the complexities of supporting is a key stage in building an effective land venture methodology. Let's investigate the financing industry and set you up for financial success in real estate.

Segment 4: Property Assurance Models for Picking Useful Speculation properties

Not all properties are made same, and picking the right one is crucial for result in land viable monetary preparation. In this part, we'll approach the major models for perceiving properties with the potential for benefit. From inspecting property condition to assessing market revenue, you'll secure pieces of information into the components that add to a productive hypothesis.

Single-Family Homes versus Multi-Unit Properties

The kind of property you pick can out and out impact your hypothesis framework and returns. The advantages and disadvantages of single-family homes versus multi-unit properties will be examined in this section. We'll discuss things like gamble, property the board, and income so you can arrive at better conclusions about your ventures in view of your inclinations and objectives.

Evaluating Neighborhoods

Your venture property's area is similarly just about as significant as the actual property. In this section, we'll guide you through the most well-known approach to evaluating neighborhoods to recognize those with strong potential for long stretch turn of events and rental interest. Factors like security, comforts, and closeness to central organizations will be covered, giving you a careful construction for going with sound hypothesis decisions.

As we navigate the complexities of property selection, keep in mind that each criterion contributes to the success of your investment as a whole. Whether you're zeroing in on a single family home or considering a multi-unit property, understanding the key factors that influence property assurance is a chief push toward building a valuable land portfolio. Could we dive into the intricacies of property assurance and set up for your advancement in the strong universe of venture property contributing?

Part 5: Property Examinations as A component of

An expected level of effort In land effective money management, careful reasonable level of investment is fundamental, and property reviews are a fundamental piece of this cycle. We'll look into the significance of thorough property assessments in this section. We'll look at the sorts of assessments you should consider, how to utilize qualified regulators, and the essential pieces of a property to overview. This data will empower you to uncover potential issues and make informed decisions before finishing up your endeavor.

Title Search and Real Considerations

Ensuring an unquestionable title is an urgent push toward the healthy amount of input process. This part will guide you through the intricacies of driving a title search, getting a handle on title security, and watching out for legal thoughts related with land trades. By quickly resolving title issues, you can protect your investment and avoid future issues.

Natural and Drafting Issues

Natural and drafting considerations can significantly influence your project's plausibility and success. We'll dive into how to recognize anticipated regular risks, investigate drafting rules, and lighten related bets. You'll be better ready to decide if a property meets your venture goals and neighborhood guidelines in the event that you comprehend these variables during the reasonable level of effort stage.

As we research the healthy amount of input process, recall that thorough assessment is a proactive measure to defend your endeavor and assurance a smooth ownership experience. From property surveys to legal thoughts, ruling the normal amount of input stage is a fundamental skill for any land monetary patron. We'd like to provide you with the information and tools you need to make sound, cost-effective decisions and make well-informed bets?

Segment 6: Working out Expected Rental

Pay by doing the math Understanding your speculation property's monetary likely beginnings with precisely ascertaining rental pay. In this section, we'll jump into the components that influence rental rates, how to lead measurable studying to choose relentless rents, and thoughts at setting ideal rental expenses. By overwhelming this point of view, you'll be arranged to grow your property's compensation potential.

Evaluating Working Expenses

A sensible assessment of working expenses is fundamental for definite money related readiness. This section will walk you through the most common method for evaluating various operational costs associated with purchasing and managing an investment property. You will figure out how to make an extensive financial plan that considers every single imaginable use, from property the executives charges to upkeep costs.

Pay Assessment

Positive pay is the foundation of powerful land monetary preparation. We'll discuss income, how to ascertain it, and why it's a significant measurement for sorting out how well your venture is doing monetarily. We will also talk about ways to improve cash flow, such as how to spend less while making more money. A solid handle of pay examination will draw in you to go with sound financial decisions and assurance the excessively long advantage of your hypothesis.

As we dive into the money related pieces of land monetary preparation, recall that exact and cautious computing is the basis of a compelling hypothesis strategy. From rental compensation calculations to pay assessment, overwhelming the financial pieces of property ownership will show you the way to money related result in the domain of speculation property contributing. Could we hop into the numbers and outfit you with the gadgets to seek after informed financial decisions for your territory portfolio.

7th Chapter: Arranging the Arrangement

Viable Exchange Procedures

Discussion is an expertise that can fundamentally influence the progress of your land exchanges. This part will investigate demonstrated exchange procedures customized to the interesting elements of land bargains. From understanding the dealer's inspirations to utilizing economic situations, you'll figure out how to arrange terms that line up with your speculation objectives and expand the worth of your buy.

Grasping the Specialty of Give and take

Land dealings frequently include split the difference. This part will dive into the specialty of tracking down commonly advantageous arrangements. We'll talk about recognizing regions where compromise is conceivable without forfeiting your center targets, encouraging positive correspondence with all gatherings included, and making shared benefit situations. Understanding how to explore and embrace compromise is a vital component of effective land discussions.

Closing the Deal

Closing a real estate deal necessitates effective coordination and careful attention to detail. In this segment, we'll direct you through the last strides of the exchange cycle. From finishing desk work to tending to potential difficulties that might emerge prior to shutting, you'll acquire bits of knowledge into guaranteeing a smooth and effective shutting. Understanding the complexities of settling the negotiation will situate you to finish exchanges with certainty.

As we investigate the specialty of discussion and arrangement conclusion, recollect that these abilities are fundamental for getting great terms as well as for building positive connections in the land business. Whether you're a carefully prepared financial backer or a novice, dominating the exchange cycle is a key stage in making progress in the serious universe of land effective money management. We should dive into powerful discussion procedures, the specialty of give and take, and the complexities of shutting arrangements to hoist your land venture.

Area 8: Property The board

DIY versus Capable Property The board

Picking whether to manage your venture property yourself or enlist capable property the board organizations is a basic choice. To help you in pursuing an educated choice in view of your own inclinations, obligation to time, and mastery, this segment will look at the benefits and drawbacks of every system. To keep up with your venture's drawn out progress, fathoming the obligations of property management is fundamental.

Occupant screening and Lease Courses of action

Quality occupants are the supporting of a viable speculation property adventure. This segment will guide you through the occupant screening process, researching strong methodologies for surveying potential tenants and directing risks. We will likewise examine the parts of areas of strength for an understanding, including significant terms and lawful contemplations to protect the two landowners and inhabitants.

Dealing with Fixes and Upkeep

Staying aware of the condition of your property is major for saving its worth and attracting quality inhabitants. We'll discuss systems for managing fixes and backing, whether you conclude to do it without any other person's assistance or select specialists. You will learn how to create a plan for proactive maintenance that covers everything from routine maintenance to dealing with unexpected repairs to ensure the longevity of your investment.

Property the board is an essential piece of venture property ownership, influencing occupant satisfaction, property assessment, and for the most part benefit. Whether you choose a Do-It-Yourself approach or enlist capable help, understanding the intricacies of property the leaders is imperative to a productive and reasonable land adventure. Could we dive into the nuances of managing your speculation property, from inhabitant screening to upkeep, and outfit you with the data to truly administer your territory portfolio.

Section 9: Making Recurring, automated revenue

Setting Serious Rental Rates

Successful rental rate setting is a foundation of creating predictable recurring, automated revenue. In this part, we'll investigate strategies for deciding serious rental rates in your market. From directing statistical surveying to understanding the elements that impact evaluating, you'll acquire experiences into setting rents that draw in quality occupants while augmenting your property's pay potential.

Boosting Inhabitance

Keeping up with high inhabitance rates is fundamental for a constant flow of recurring, automated revenue. We'll examine methodologies for drawing in and holding occupants, including successful advertising, occupant maintenance programs, and responsive property the board. You will be in a better position to keep your units occupied and generate dependable rental income if you implement these strategies.

Methodologies for Expanding Rental Pay

Past setting cutthroat leases and expanding inhabitance, there are extra methodologies for expanding your rental pay. This part will investigate techniques, for example, esteem added upgrades, investigating elective revenue sources (e.g., pet charges, clothing offices), and enhancing lease arrangements. You can increase the overall profitability of your portfolio of rental properties by implementing these strategies.

Keep in mind that a planned and proactive approach is essential to long-term financial success as we look into passive income generation. Whether you're another financial backer or an accomplished landowner, understanding how to set serious rents, keep up with high inhabitance, and execute pay supporting techniques will add to the drawn out thriving of your land ventures. How about we investigate the methodologies for making recurring, automated revenue and boosting the monetary capability of your investment properties.

Part 10: Tax Strategies for Real Estate Investors

Understanding Tax Deductions Maximizing returns from real estate investing necessitates maximizing your tax position. This part will investigate the different assessment derivations accessible to land financial backers, including allowances for contract revenue, property the board charges, fixes, and that's only the tip of the iceberg. Understanding how to use these allowances will assist you with limiting your available pay and upgrade the general benefit of your venture.

Deterioration Advantages

Deterioration is an integral asset that can give huge duty benefits to land financial backers. In this section, we'll dig into the idea of deterioration, how it applies to land, and the advantages it offers with regards to lessening available pay. Understanding how to compute and apply devaluation will add to long haul charge effectiveness and monetary outcome in your land tries.

Working with a Land Bookkeeper

Exploring the intricacies of land tax collection frequently requires the mastery of an expert. We'll talk about why it's important to work with a real estate accountant who understands the special tax issues associated with property ownership. From choosing a certified bookkeeper to teaming up on charge arranging methodologies, you'll acquire experiences into how a learned proficient can be a significant resource for your land speculation venture.

As we investigate charge systems for land financial backers, remember that proactive expense arranging can significantly affect your main concern. Whether you're a beginner financial backer or a carefully prepared land owner, understanding the subtleties of expense derivations, deterioration benefits, and the job of a land bookkeeper will enable you to pursue informed monetary choices and boost your after-government forms. Let's get into the world of tax strategies and put you in a good position to make money from real estate investments.

Area 11: The Influence of Appreciation in Creating Long hauls financial wellbeing

Land appreciation can possibly be a huge supporter of long haul riches. We'll discuss the possibility of appreciation, how it occurs in the housing business sector, and how to track down properties with a great deal of potential for appreciation in this segment. Your land portfolio's overall development and your total assets will improve over time if you know how to use appreciation.

Using Worth

Esteem is a significant asset that can be used to develop your territory adventure portfolio. In this section, we'll look at how value works over time, how to find it, and the risks and benefits of using your property's value. By truly using esteem, you can accelerate your growing a significant monetary establishment outing and capitalize on new pursuit open entryways.

Leave Frameworks

Having a particular leave method is imperative for long stretch advancement in land cash the board. We'll research different leave strategies, including selling for benefit, 1031 exchanges, and changing to standoffish ownership. You will be able to take advantage of economic conditions, reduce risks, and decisively position your portfolio for supported development if you know when and how to implement your leave system.

As we dive into making long stretch monetary energy through land, recall that result in this attempt requires a blend of key planning, market understanding, and financial wisdom. Whether you're basically starting your hypothesis interaction or expecting to refine your approach, getting a handle on the power of appreciation, using esteem, and completing reasonable leave strategies will clear a path for upheld financial achievement. We should look into ways to build long-term financial stability through your land ventures.

12th Section: Risk The board Directing Risks in Land Cash the board

Risk is natural in land monetary preparation, but effective bet the leaders can shield your hypothesis. We'll look at proactive systems for identifying and reducing risks associated with property ownership in this section. You'll learn about risk assessment and mitigation strategies that will help protect your venture portfolio, from market risks to property-specific issues.

Protection Considerations Protection is an essential component of land hazards. The property protection, obligation protection, and landowner protection that are applicable to land owners will be examined top to bottom in this part. Understanding the nuances of insurance policies will empower you to make informed decisions to defend your assets and moderate likely financial incidents.

Managing Astonishing Hardships

Land successful monetary arranging is dynamic, and unanticipated troubles can arise. This part will guide you through strategies for managing surprising circumstances, for instance, financial downturns, property damage, or inhabitant issues. By making crisis game-plans and knowing how to answer challenges, you'll be more ready to investigate the weaknesses of land powerful monetary preparation with adaptability and sureness.

Remember that the most ideal way to stay away from issues is to be proactive and ready as we check out in danger the executives in land. Whether you're a painstakingly arranged monetary patron or new to the real estate market, understanding how to assess and direct bets, picking fitting security consideration, and investigating astounding troubles will add to the long advancement and flexibility of your hypothesis portfolio. We should take a gander at far to successfully oversee risk while putting resources into land.

Part 13: Scaling Your Portfolio

Differentiating Your Speculations

Enhancement is a major procedure for relieving risk and improving the general solidness of your land portfolio. We will discuss the significance of diversifying your investments across various property types, locations, and market segments in this section. Understanding how to make a differentiated portfolio will situate you to weather conditions market vacillations and upgrade your general returns.

Funding Systems for Extension

Scaling your land portfolio frequently includes key supporting. This section will dive into funding systems for extending your portfolio, including utilizing existing value, investigating innovative supporting choices, and grasping the effect of obligation on your speculation procedure. By dominating funding techniques, you can open doors for development and exploit good economic situations.

Building a Land Speculation Portfolio

Building an effective land venture portfolio requires cautious preparation and execution. We'll talk about the standards of portfolio development, including laying out venture objectives, choosing properties that line up with your system, and improving the general execution of your portfolio. Whether you're holding back nothing, capital appreciation, or a blend of both, understanding how to construct an enhanced and key portfolio is critical to long haul achievement.

As you leave on the excursion of scaling your land portfolio, remember that essential direction and an exhaustive comprehension of market elements are fundamental. The principles of diversification, financing strategies, and portfolio construction will guide you in building a resilient and successful real estate investment portfolio, whether you are an experienced investor looks to expand or a newcomer entering the market. How about we investigate the systems for scaling your portfolio and accomplishing you're drawn out venture goals.

End

Congrats on finishing this aide on investment property contributing! As you consider the abundance of data gave, we should recap a few vital focus points and diagram your subsequent stages for an effective land venture.

Recap of Key Action items

- Figuring out the Essentials: Land effective financial planning includes key procurement and the executives of properties to create pay and create financial stability.

- Market Study: To find profitable markets and make educated investment decisions, thorough market research and analysis are essential.

- Supporting Basics: Investigating contract choices, understanding loan fees, and exploring the advance endorsement process are basic moves toward getting the right supporting for your venture.

- Property Choice: Measures for choosing beneficial properties, picking between single-family homes and multi-unit properties, and assessing neighborhoods are essential to fruitful property determination.

- An expected level of investment: Property reviews, title look, and tending to ecological and drafting issues are essential parts of a reasonable level of investment prior to finishing any land exchange.

- Doing the math: For financial planning and maximizing profitability, it is essential to conduct a cash flow analysis, estimate operating expenses, and calculate potential rental income.

- Discussion Abilities: Compelling discussion procedures, grasping the craft of give and take, and settling the negotiation are basic for effective land exchanges.

- Property The executives: Settling on Do-It-Yourself and expert property the board, occupant screening, rent arrangements, and taking care of fixes and support are key parts of powerful property the executives.

- Making Automated revenue: Setting serious rental rates, expanding inhabitance, and executing systems for expanding rental pay add to making a solid stream of automated revenue.

- Charge Techniques: Working with a real estate accountant and comprehending tax deductions are essential for maximizing your tax position.

- Building Wealth Over Time: Building long-term wealth through real estate necessitates utilizing equity, appreciation, and clearly defined exit strategies.

- Risk The executives: Protecting your investment and ensuring long-term success necessitates taking insurance into account, reducing risks, and overcoming unexpected obstacles.

- Scaling Your Portfolio: Broadening your ventures, investigating supporting techniques for development, and building a land speculation portfolio are critical to scaling and developing your riches.

- Subsequent stages for Your Land Process
- Evaluate Your Objectives: Return to your speculation objectives and guarantee they line up with the procedures and bits of knowledge acquired from this aide.

- Make a move: Execute the information obtained into your land adventures. Whether you're a beginner or experienced financial backer, making a move is critical for progress.

- Learned: Land is dynamic, and kept learning is critical to remaining ahead. Investigate progressed subjects, go to studios, and organization with individual financial backers.

- Network and Work together: Join neighborhood land venture gatherings, go to industry occasions, and interface with experts. Systems administration can open ways to important open doors and bits of knowledge.

- Examine and modify: Consistently audit your portfolio, monetary objectives, and economic situations.

Be ready to change your procedures in view of developing conditions.

- Keep in mind that real estate investing is a journey that necessitates perseverance, diligence, and ongoing education. By applying the standards and methodologies illustrated in this aide, you're strategically set up for outcome in the powerful universe of investment property contributing. Good luck on your land process!

www.ingramcontent.com/pod-product-compliance
Lightning Source LLC
Chambersburg PA
CBHW072327270726
48658CB00016B/2055